Out Pondered the Hare

Poetry

By Steven W. Simon

Fourth Edition, February 2023

ISBN: 979-8-3484-8049-3

www.stevensimonbooks.com

For Whitney.

In remembrance:
Marcus F, Matthew N, David L,
Nathan F, Ryan G

Pearly Whites

We lined the boys against the wall –
this one's got balls,
he got moxie.
Cappuccino hand – cell phone wrist.
That grin, lord almighty we know that
grin.
Ignore his suit pants.
Ignore everything past his
Pearly Whites.
Love me no wrong – love me
virility and polished shoes
old age grows – a mansion.
Captivated by the interior. Felt up by
dollar bills
By strippers
By aides
By girls walking home from school.

No worries, no worries.

Raptured on earth
Raptured now
Raptured around
Heathens poor
Food stamps numbered on budgets.
Ignore everything
past his Pearly Whites — we lined the

boys against the wall
this one's got moxie
He goes first.

Waiting for a Funeral

Frank bellows – inaudible.
The doctor: yes, a broken hip.
Left shoulder dislocated.
How has his diet been?
Is there a doctor we can speak to?
Medical history?
Should we use soft restraints?
Did you let him urinate

into paper towels
and then set them aside?

"He likes catfish nuggets," Frank's
wife
expected that
And only that
to satisfy every question.

The ER liaison stepped out into the
lobby
periodically.
Hispanic and young, a gut starting
under
his button-down collared shirt; green
with white stripes.

The obese in the waiting room knew
he was gay.
The skinny – who had brought the
obese – also knew and they stared.

"At Saint Mary's,
like all other hospitals,
the emergency room sees patients
based on seriousness of your
problem,"
a slight lisp.
Spoke over "SportsCenter"
overworked lungs hungry for air
through the fat.
An African-American woman raised
her hand,
her body squeezed into a lobby chair.
The ER liaison walked over.
She pointed to her husband,
asleep in a hospital wheelchair.
The ER Liaison was in charge of coffee
and tea;
you had to ask for it.
He never allowed the obese to have
any.

Frank ripped his IV lines
tried to stand.
The nurse was sick of him

later described him on charts as
dementia.
The doctors pumped him full
morphine;
the nurse retreated
the loading dock for a cigarette.
Frank went limp and snored
through his toothless mouth.
A new doctor
Black, young and tall with thin-
rimmed glasses.
X-rays.
Indeed a broken hip.
The wife had left for supper.
A dislocated shoulder.
Lab results. Diabetes and blood
poisoned – inconclusive.
Morphine dreams
of being home with the blind dog he
screamed,
guttural noises – toothless.
The comfort of cat urine ammonia and
dust floated rooms,
side-stepping antique soda cans and
picture frames.
He loved that dog: that blind dog that
shot out from under his legs
for a squirrel and caused his fall.
Loved that house even when "the
blacks" started "ruining [inaudible]."

If he had the energy he would
continue to hoard.

"Why are we in New York?" Frank
asked the nurse who had grown to
understand him.
"We are not in New York, we are in
Illinois," replied the young black
woman.
He tried to stand and she pressed a
button. Frank went limp.
"The soybeans, Pa needs me out there
with the soybeans."
"We are not in Alabama," the nurse
said, "we are in Illinois."
Frank swallowed hard and tried to
focus through milky fog.
"Okay."
"Now you stay where you're at, you
hear me?"

Frank looked around the room as he
tried to move his limbs past the soft
restraints around his wrists and
ankles. Milky fog.
"Okay," he said to her in a soft moan.
"We'll have you patched up in no time
Mr. Frank." Frank looked away and

toward the window, the sun shown
brightly and he could tell.
"Baseball today?"
The nurse took the television remote
and flipped through several channels.
She placed the remote in his hand and
moved his index finger onto the
volume buttons.
"This is volume up," she slid his finger
down, "and this is volume down."
She left the room as Frank let his head
sink into the pillow. The Cubs were
down by two in the eighth.

Yellowed Feathers Lurch

Abrasive lilac
The Suburbs
On High
Abrasive finch
Yellowed feathers lurch
Crooked wing cracked
Through heat on past
On High
Grafted skin under beak
Though she conceded
Adored
Fell Through
Unconditional
Yellowed feathers
Lurch
Finches born
The Suburbs
On High

Truthfully, I Intend to be Truthful

I've been thinking about suicide
Since Heather.
Not in the traditional sense,
nor was Heather the catalyst
– simply bad timing.

Not with a gun, of which I don't own.
Nor a knife
Truthfully, and I intend to be truthful
I have slid the dull spline against my
wrists
on numerous occasions
but have yet to invert and set
the blade to my skin.

Perhaps arrogance that my thoughts
go to accidental.
That I yearn for it,
for the drunk driver to swerve.
The bank robber to use me.
cancer to destroy my insides as my
mother and father tell me to stay
strong
and then weep as they walk to the car
in the hospital parking garage.

Former classmates line up at my casket
and lament
Impossible through self-infliction, and
therefore
I avoid those hypotheticals.

It's in that moment,
the seconds before sleep,
that it is most real and I hold
my breath.

The others.

Alan whose pickup truck rolled over on
the highway, ejected him halfway out
the window shattering the glass and
the top of the cab crushed down on his
skull. His mother insisted on an open
casket, of which the funeral director
reluctantly obliged. Having seen the
attempt at reconstruction I have
concluded that he must have pushed
back.

Fred found with a needle in his arm
next to a boy I didn't know. Patrick
whose heart gave out after rehab didn't
take. Natalia who, as a passenger, was
killed by her drunk friend in the
driver's seat.

We pined, sure.

We lamented the losses and grieved in
our own ways.

Pinned green and gold ribbons on our
suits, lead the caskets to the hearses
and followed them smoking cigarettes
with our hazard lights flashing to the
cemeteries.

Too young,
we told each other.
Yet it dawned
each of us had made similar decisions
yet were designated pall bearers.
Witnesses to the grieving mothers
and fathers
and each other.

We had all been that drunk driver, that
passenger. One who had snorted or put
acid on their tongue. It would be nice
to think of our times at the funeral
homes as stark reminders of the
choices we've made, of decisions made
in contrast to logic or reasoning. But
we knew that we wouldn't change, that
we wouldn't stop.

We believed in luck too strongly,
and the hedonistic draw
was too much for us
to overcome.

Perhaps that's what drew us together
as friends
and what returns us often to the places
in which we grieve.

Los Angeles Murder

Los Angeles Murder
Sunset
Vine
Hobo coffee conversation
Dry morning
Arid November
Hobo dumps on front lawn
Ethereal Hollywood
He smiles
Behind the tree
Del Taco supper
Cat urine carpet
Wretched
400 pounds recliner lurches
Pounds the wall
House shutters
Settles
Settles
Del Taco supper
Chocolate and 2% milk in a bed
Ikea cheap metal bars
Fat African squats
Urinates
Hollywood
Highland

Piss – Piss – Piss
Walking steadily to drink
Out West he regrets
Can't shake it
Can't shake it

Splatter the City in Ghetto

God Damn It! He Screamed!
Gripped rails as there entered Death
Rider
Antique Shop rummage through
typewriters
Ribbons cut with a baseball Bat
Antithesis purveyor of goods
Where children stepped out to alleys
Felt their first Steel
First grip of Death Riding
For Protection! He whispered to
Children
Though not now
Not Now
Death Rider has the edge
And he Swings and he Swings
Antithesis Purveyor of goods
Flattened on peeled tile
Gripped with blood
Breathe slow Purveyor of antiques
Shop nestled betwixt the Ghetto
Before
There was Ghetto
Breathe slow Father
As the son of the purveyor bullied

Whilst schooled will summon
Courage of the Rage of a teenage boy
Acne forceful shoved in lockers by
jocks
By lesser jocks
The son of the purveyor will eye the
Death Rider
Spectacle suit black juried peers
And he will eye
And he will Think
When they First Felt that Steel
When this here was not whilst
schooled
That revenge on the ghetto that now
surrounds
Abandoned antique shops
Nails salons creeping weeds
Splatter the city in Ghetto

Dawn, Suburban Detroit

Sitting outside my apartment door with a beer, I'm twenty now. The sun comes up over the courtyard. Across the way a man murdered his wife. Two doors down to the right a gaggle of Goth kids, a toddler and video games. To my left sleeps a German college student who reads cookbooks at the beach. My roommate left for rehab a week ago after a night involving a naked obese woman slapped with a limp penis, a National Geographic magazine featuring otters, random maple syrup bottles and the denial of urination on a couch.

I spent the last three nights in a funeral home, I'm twenty now. I was a production assistant on a low-budget short film featuring a dead body in an embalming room. I smoked a lot of cigarettes and sat in the room with the couches and facial tissues everywhere. I got home around six every morning and I'd sit outside and drink a beer.

The Goth girl was a manager at a
Starbucks, she hired me as a barista.
The man was convicted of murdering
his wife. The German student went
back to Germany. My roommate is
doing alright I hear. I'm twenty-one
now.

Puckers

She puckers over stale coffee
First snow radiator hiss
Exhaling cigarette through window
cracked
Blond third floor walk-up
Blond three block walk
To the train
Blond secure in Yoga pants
Alumni hoodie
Three months in the city
Radiator hiss
Snow on the windowsill

The Girls I've
Married

I remember the stench of the
basement
the sweaty dancers made up
Abercrombie and Tommy Hilfiger
gripped cans.
She followed me up the narrow
staircase
out of the human heat
humidity that hung comfortably
clinging to our clothes in false
religious glow - our cheeks
glossy eyes until we feel
our beliefs wait patiently for the
darkness of our laughter.
It was a Wednesday
had we the converts
in their entirety, to wreck havoc?
Through the abused glass door
It's closure slammed on exit and into
the intrusive
melee of smokers covered in winter
coats
the rotten moon thick and I stuck my
eyes
into its insistent haloed parody

My pupils neared as if I was the one
creating.
Through pockets for a cigarette and
felt
her presence
Stuck out my arm with a second
smoke
met with a relaxed hand seeking to
know my reaction
of her other fingers mute
A gentlemen
and I lit her tip.
John came and reminded
- don't sit on the couch
- don't watch TV
- keep your hands out of your pockets
The frigid air
near the chain link fence
and watched her writer her name and
phone number
on a scrap of paper
Reminded me again of where she will
be
and when -
I was hungry and didn't care much for
her voice.
Two girls stood in the kitchen
blonde
the shorter one wore gold-rimmed
glasses, the taller

heavy lipstick and her arms crossed
”public relations” she answered
”finance” and I asked her what that
meant
I don't remember the answer
waste of time, I thought.
She hugged me
said goodbye and I forgot her
Not because I disliked her
But how could I expect to mature
knowing I would use her
In the end.
I'd like to tell you about the girls
I've married
Divorced the moment they sober up
About the girls who say "you're cute"
Reciprocity with sweaty palms
Mind towards safe harbor
Ashore
His pupils intimidated by dark clouds
Peaceful on the horizon.

As he Espoused Evangelical to an Agreeable Mother

A dance academy waiting room.
Plush black leather chairs. She was tall,
of Dutch features
and South African origin.
He too, was tall. That evangelical smile
that hid something as he espoused evangelical
to an agreeable mother.
His tight black bicycle pants that
angered me more.
Her child in all pink
coloring within the lines.
His child in all pink watching.
"You know," she started,
"when Nelson Mandela was elected,"
and she paused, looked at the color of my skin,
at his,
and at hers before continuing,
"it was awful. It ruined everything.
And we, the [white] South Africans
left. For New Zealand. For here."

"What about Jews?" he asked.
"No Jews," she answered. "No Jews."
Evangelicals,
they always have to slide us into a
conversation.

My Indian Girlfriend

Stripped of quiet confidence
my Indian girlfriend has locked
herself
in the bathroom
The boy has kept a record
of pizzas
soda cans
he's slipped through the window
seen her nude - masturbated in his
rusted
'87 Ford Escort
I sat down by the door saturated
by the day
The locksmith came and after hearing
her voice considered it a sin
Gave him a Bud Light and he set to
explaining
nay - demanding more beer
pornography for his troubles.
Without clothes his obesity was
overwhelming
and she shot him dead whilst I
napped
dropped the pink towel and made
footprints as she walked

took my hand
led me to the bathroom
and locked the door.

Mario Kart Instructions: Playing Against a 4-year-old Boy

A request to play the "racing game"
can come at any time.
Even during a football game.
Be prepared.
A DVR is a necessity - you will be
playing Mario Kart
in less than five minutes.
If there are two chairs, one of normal,
adult size and the other - child size
with no cushion
you will be relegated to the child's
chair.
Think of it as a real-life go-kart
simulation
as your ass falls asleep.
Sure, the couch is comfortable
but you have been instructed
otherwise.
You do not get first pick of characters.
Ever.

Explain that some cars only go with
certain characters
at your own peril.
The child will insist on a specific
course,
you cannot play Grand Prix mode.
In versus mode -
You do not get to pick the course.
Ever.
You will be going backwards to avoid
winning.
The child will eventually figure this
out
Apologize
turn around
and fall off ledges for the next three
minutes
until you are in 2nd place.
Once you have successfully navigated
to solid second,
proceed to shoot shells, lighting bolts,
whatever
at your child's kart.
No mercy. No quarter.
It is in this situation
and only this situation
that you are allowed to loudly and
obnoxiously
talk smack to a 4-year-old.

Congratulate the child with a high-
five
and a sense of awe when he wins.
At any point
the game may be halted
for a potty break.
The child will sprint to the bathroom.
Do not be tempted to unpause the
game.
Your phone, if handy, is an excellent
way
to pass the time.
If the child screams from across the
house
you will need to wipe his butt.
Wash hands, return to game.
Spend some time searching
for hidden passageways.
If you are going retro
you are forbidden from exploiting
the N64 ice course glitch.
You are allowed to win
but at the end
your record must be under .500.
Tread carefully -
the child may, at any point, decide this
is over.
At this time it may seem that you are
allowed
to play Mario Kart by yourself

at 150cc
in Grand Prix mode.
This is wrong - the child has decided
this is over, for everyone.

Paid in Prague Meditation

They were prancing
paid in Prague meditation.
Segued into eternal discussion
background in bronze
and candy fashions.
　　　　His morning Tao.
Only human for a flu-like
fiscal year
on drivel.

Three miles to Padilla's
and blameless.
That Manhattan Dom,
her injuries in service
to living presidents
That Manhattan Active Army
Licked up looking like Police.
　　　　30 cc's,
　　　　　the Market police.
The granddaddy of Bomb
the only bipartisan rat Dickens
a knot that stores
alone the mind to be fulfilled
And from us God
not to give to the kind.

The Man Henry Aashish

The accuracy of Mbuji-Mayi
with a sure foot fall
The comment that man made earlier
The man Henry Aashish.
His clothes on the floor
is the story rendered true?
is the Mandarin accurate
and the promise the same in Madrid?

Bert the Turtle

They put us under our desks after
recess
Had us count to 30
we did it slowly, to ourselves,
the soft whisper of 1st graders
who had yet to master their inner
voices
The day after they brought the
television
into the classroom
on a wheeled cart
We watched the Challenger
and before the debris had fallen back
to earth she unplugged the television
and wheeled it out
and they put us under our desks
had us count to 30.

A Technique for Slurpee

I met Alice at one in the morning
7-Eleven. Both cotton-mouthed and
craving.
She pulled the lever and the slippery
half-liquid, half-solid sugary drink
fell into her paper cup. I watched her
as the bright red overflowed
and ran down the side of the cup.

I put the lid on first.
Positioned the lid a millimeter
from the spout,
deftly held the cup and held the lever
until three-quarters full.
Knocked the bottom against the
counter three times

the contents settled.

"There's a technique to it," I told her,
too stoned to flirt or realize she had
maybe started flirting with me.
"The lid goes on first, otherwise you
don't get all you paid for.
            Gotta fill it three-quarters

give a good three taps
      the liquid from the start gets
mixed in with the frozen and then
finish pouring."

13 Mile and Woodward

They all looked like doctors.
Lab coats with cursive writing
stitched
"MD" included in the blue thread over
white.
Yes, they were all doctors.
She told me to see someone after we
broke up. Someone who could help.
After she stopped sending letters, the
ones handwritten
that started with how much she
missed me and segued into events
she found interesting.
Her first experiences at the
university.
The first snow which always came
early
in the Upper Peninsula. An interesting
professor.
How she missed her horses and then,
again,
how she missed me,
how she loved me,
and then signed with a heart over the
"i."

I could smell her chestnut hair when I
opened the envelopes,
decorated in multicolored pen.
Of hearts.
Rainbows and XOXOs.
No,
I couldn't smell the Aussie shampoo
and Marlboro menthol cigarette
smoke.
I couldn't smell it.
She told me to see someone. Someone
who could help.
It was not her decision
a number torn from a bookstore
bulletin board of cork and
thumbtacks.
Surely, I'm not too big to admit she
was my first love
and that I was definitely hurt by the
rejection,
as would anyone.
She had rejected me several times
before I called the psychic hotline and
took me
to drink cheap coffee and smoke
cigarettes
into the morning brought by a
waitress one mistake from stripping.
Told me that she loved me,
told me I was the first one she said

that to and
her virginity.
I set the letters on fire in the backyard
between
two and four am on a weekday
and remembered how afraid I was to
meet her mother,
her father.
I'm almost positive they were all
doctors. It was an oddity
that my palms were not sweaty.
My heart ignored that deep, inverse
beat
that seemed to pause
before it raced ungodly
fast.
No tingling that starts in my inner
thighs
worked its way up my torso
punches me in the lungs.
Everything was fine. Everything is
fine.
I think this used to be a pediatrician's
office.
The outline of ABCs along the edge of
the walls
Associated animals painted over.
G for giraffe.
Z for zebra.

Do all children cry when they get
shots?
Did I cry?
Was I comforted by my mother's
reassurance that the pain was, in the
end, good for me?
I'm sure, it was a pediatrician's office.
D for dog.
Mr. Marx, she said.
At nineteen I still looked young,
maybe fifteen.
I can't remember now,
hours later,
if my voice had cracked.
I think she was a nurse.
maroon scrubs and a stethoscope.
Any family history of heart disease?
Yes.
Cancer?
Yes.
Diabetes?
No.
Have you been tested for HIV?
No.
Do you smoke?
Yes.
Do you drink?
Yes.
Do you do drugs? No.

Sign this.
What's the date? The twentieth.
August, right?
Yes. August 20, 1998.
She wrapped the blood pressure cuff.
I saw down her shirt and blushed
Her cleavage and the subconscious
innuendo of the cuff
tightening around my appendage.
Her Pantene auburn hair felt like
cheating on Aussie
Yes, she was a nurse,
deep breaths,
cold metal on my back and she left.
I checked my palms again, still dry.
Two coats?
Or maybe
taken off the letters and the animals.
I followed a girl once
who beckoned at midnight onto a
school bus
parked behind a church.
I touched her breasts and when we left
I stole
the letter E stuck above the windows
with tape
and the bus driver's bible.
Mr. Marx, he said
felt naked without a lab coat
nor scrubs.

Balding
made up for it with a full beard. A tie
so he must be important. He sat
down,
crossed a leg over the other
his own clipboard.
What is your ancestry?
Eastern European.
Jew?
Yes.
Are you in school?
No.
Why not?
I don't know.
Do you work?
Yes.
Doing what?
I'm a barista.
A what?
I make coffee.
Did you graduate high school?
Yes.
What was your grade point average?
I don't remember exactly.
Ballpark it.
I don't know, two, two point five.
Closer to two or closer to two point
five?
Maybe between the two.

Let's say two point five, are your
parents still married?
Yes.
Are you nervous right now?
A little.
Hmm. He wrote something on the
paper.
What does your father do?
He teaches.
Teaches what?
Math.
Are you good at math?
No.
And your mother?
She's a teacher too. English.
Are you good at English?
A little.
Do you live with them?
No.
Why not?
I just don't.
Where do you live?
In an apartment.
With whom?
A roommate.
Do you have siblings?
No.
What is your sexual preference?
I'm straight.

Have you ever deviated?
Deviated?
Strayed, had a homosexual
encounter.
No.
He flipped the paper over the
clipboard.
I'm going to say a word and I want
you to say the first word that comes to
your mind, do you understand?
Yes.
Table.
Chair.
Moon.
Stars.
Cat.
Dog.
Chair.
Table.
Football.
Baseball.
Driving.
Passenger.
Book.
Notebook.
Tree.
Leaf.
I've thought about returning the bible
The letter E is mine, forever.

He handed me a pad of white paper
Wm. Sullivan & Son Funeral Directors
written across the top
near the yellow glue.
Write down any friends that would
benefit from our services.
Your services?
Yes, why you are here, I'm sure there
are others you could recommend.
I don't think, I mean my situation
Isn't special. Write at least one friend,
please.
Is the nurse coming back, after you?
I don't believe so, why do you ask?
No reason.
Write.
I have to go back
Tuesday at nine thirty in the morning
a large Black nurse yelled at me to get
dressed and leave.
11 Mile on Woodward
stuck at a light I felt the tingle in my
thighs and my hands slid
I moved them to the bottom of the
steering wheel.
I focused on my breathing
disavowed the dripping cherry red
plastic as it slid
over the passenger-side vent
dribbled onto the carpet.

I looked out my window and tried so
hard
to imagine what her life in her car was
like.
She's married,
two young children who will make her
proud someday.
Murder her in her sleep. One a doctor,
the other a star athlete.
A quarterback. Shot up the school.
Called in a bomb threat like Lucas
to get his girlfriend out of a math test
on a Friday afternoon and had to call
three times
because no one does that.
No one shoots up a school, no one
bombs a school.
So hard.
Green light
the cassette deck flipped the side
click
and I drove straight,
forty-six and 2 got to the apartment
building around four pm.
David wasn't home yet,
at least his car wasn't there.
The seatbelt caught but I didn't care
stumbled to the dry bushes and
vomited.

Woke in the parking lot on cracked tar
still daylight.
A shard from a broken bottle stuck to
my arm,
I pulled it out and it didn't bleed too
much and I wiped the dirt from the
cut.
I closed the car door and it clunked
because the seatbelt was stuck on the
latch.
David's car has a plastic bag taped
where the rear window should be. He
was sleeping with a girl who, until she
was twelve, lived in England. She
didn't have an accent, at least not one
I heard, but she decided to revive it
mid sexual session and David told her
to stop so she threw a brick through
his car window.
She's single now.
The stairs were outside the apartment
building
at the third-floor landing yellow police
tape from when he murdered her.
I did not know them
the police did not ask us any
questions.
The fifth to our apartment and it was
unlocked.
The shower running

A line cook at Big Boy and found the
smell of grease
of oil revolting
He loved to cook.
I rinsed the vomit from the corners
of my mouth
in the kitchen sink.
Aussie shampoo and menthol
cigarettes.
An "i" dotted with
a heart.
My reflection in a silvery pan
I'm the next Jim Morrison
mother fuckers.
Distorted lips
on machined metal.
An American Poet.

Shitty Coffee

Corner booth in the back of
Berkley Coney Island.
It's perception, you know.
It's shitty coffee at home but here you
don't know.
I could ask what kind it is.
Why would you do that to yourself?
The waitress knew us.
A month since George died.
Boycotted his epilepsy medication
had a seizure somewhere between
here and Grayling
on I-75. Snow. His forest green
Bonneville spun out
ended up facing the wrong way
Heard it was a Peterbilt.
The waitress took the third cup back
to the kitchen.
Put it back on the rack.
She did it slowly.
No appetites just coffee.
Those who knew him had not yet
reached a consensus.
An intentional act to mitigate this
life?
Others countered
that had he had those feelings he

would not have endangered others in
such a way.
Perhaps upbringing – his father who
loved marijuana and pornography.
His mother – spent her time snorting
cocaine in Key West.
She would return and snort 222s
offer them to us children
spit on the carpet after her saliva
dribbled
into the bong and she passed it to
some unlucky
A week, maybe two at a time, she
would be a mother.

An old man's hand shook
as he tried to pour syrup on his
pancakes
the sticky brown dripped onto a
National Geographic magazine.
Mr. Mazar,
the waitress said,
you don't have to be proud around
me,
and she took his hand gently in hers
and moved it in a circular pattern over
the pancakes.
He looked up at her and I could not
tell if his faith was restored or if he
wanted to boycott his medication. She

had never spoken to us like that. So
soft, so warm that I would have
acquiesced to her pouring my syrup
and I would have looked up at her like
a child who knew nothing. Jake saw it
too and told me later that he wanted
to add the remaining bills from his
wallet to her tip but it would have
been too awkward to return to the
booth. Next time, he promised himself
aloud to me.

The Colombian Boy
he Called Pedro

The door shut and the sun was bright
and it took several moments to
recompose from fluorescent.
I lit a cigarette and walked to the side
of the building
the cars parked.
The traffic light red.
An Impala with tinted windows
chrome rims
twelve's in the trunk.
Maybe fifteen's.
A Taurus honked at an F150 who in
turn flipped him off and told him to
fuck off.
The Impala paid no mind. I sat on my
trunk for a minute and finished my
Marlboro.
A promise of money earmarked for
community college A need to not be
homeless.
The rekindling of embarrassment.
Calling her mother Auntie when there
was no precedent
and they all laughed.

When I passed by her house, craned
my neck and saw her on a porch.
Reversed only to crash into a car
parked at the curb.
Picking a fight with the Chaldeans
hiding as a coward
when they came to finish.
I took a long last drag and flicked the
lit butt to the pavement.
Sat down on the grass embankment
I just wanted to be home
to know my nature.

His Father's Antique Shop

Behind his father's antique shop
A heavy revolver, probably a well-
known brand
I know nothing of guns.
I remember the alley more so than the
weapon.
The overgrowth that originated in the
gravel.
The quiet.
The run-down fence line.
They came to rob his father.
Bang. Bang.
That was the gun.
Self-defense, said the judge.
Vengeance, they screamed in a musty
basement. Closed the distance
and took to him with baseball bats.
Left my grandfather's violins as they
bolted
into the alley
the overgrowth
The Quiet.

Neon Snake, Coiled

Neon snake, coiled up he went
around
the elm tree trunk
 slithered
 his aqua essence born striped
 and there was ethereal orange
and the women who seance atop the
roots
basked in his glow
 scowled at the fair-haired boy
 as he flicked a cigarette into
the lawn
and the snake's head rose off the bark
as the ember lit about the blades and
the boy
hurried inside
 found the bathroom and fell
limp
at the toilet
gashed his head against
the countertop adjacent
 was nursed who pity man as
women
 who had heard the screams of
others

　　　and alit from roots
held paper towel to his forehead
M.N. tattooed on her wrist
and when crimson replaced with
another
sat him down on the beige leather
couch
　　　next to me
set his head back
wet towels to slow the warm life
leaving
and when his hue returned left him
next to me
for the roots and the ethereal orange
hit me – he beckoned and I ignored
Hit me! He echoed deep
And turned to meet my eyes
hit me, he whispered
I'm fucked up – he confessed
stood
walked out of the room
and he was gone.

Autumn Crisp

Autumn crisp and opium sweet
Cougars in Target Branded
Toting teenage daughters through
Oh this is cute
Leading cleavage by example
Touting Yoga tightness
Agape in housewares
Flustered in dairy
Pocket your wedding rings
Plead for autumn crispness
Fall fashions forward
Relieved erections
Opium sweetness that masks arousal

I am not Mr. Pritchard

Rectangle spectacles over scanning
eyes seeking weakness
Pressed pinstripe dark liquor
networking amongst peers
Amongst rectangle spectacles

Gelled hair walked 1.2 miles negative
15 wind chill negative 30
Gray slacks sports jacket lager
networking amid strangers
Amid misguided ambition

Thank you for your business card
We'll talk
What do you do?
I could really use your services
Great idea

Borne of Summer Optimism

Pot marked scars gilded lines my
mind
Ever morn custom built curses sans
invocations within Aquarius
horoscopes
Fools become pin-holed pupil abusers
of body
Fools accosted by innate failure
Ever morn fed by Arabica nicotine
dreary
Winter returns where all failures are
consecrated
Borne of summer optimism
Shown only as truth in the first white
covering

This American Dream Pure

I don't remember India, save for the stench and noise. I was too young, only five when we came to America. We moved into a small apartment in the suburbs.

> Not for lack of wealth,
> my father was determined
> that this American Dream
> pure.

My two older sisters shared a bedroom, my parents had theirs and the third was reserved for the gods, the puja room. My room was not a room at all, but a cot that I had to fold and push back behind the kitchen table every morning. Not like an army cot, it had a mattress and wasn't all that bad.

> My father's company
> little league games
> Christmas trees

Collared shirts and khaki pants

Yet the curry aroma remained, embedded in the linens and the clothes even through multiple washes. It's that, more than anything, that keeps an Indian assimilated and yet tethered to home, regardless of how regularly one returns.

My mother doted
eternal love.
Indifferent and wore a sari
Her bindi.
Her collection of VHS tapes.

One night I woke on my cot in the kitchen to find him at the kitchen table in the darkness. He was sipping a cup of tea. I closed my eyes but keep them open slightly and watched him. At that young age I had learned anger, jealousy, sadness, but I had yet to learn *this* sadness, this despair. The next night, or several later, I woke again and saw him sitting there. With his tea and morose about his face. I sat up on the cot and stared back and I remember the light from the apartment wall coming through the window blinds. He stood up and walked over to me and pet my hair. "Soon, you will have your own room, my son. With all the toys you could ever want. And we'll have a yard to play catch, and we'll put a basketball hoop in the driveway. Soon."

> Just an Indian boy
> with a crush on a Catholic girl
> straddled rejection and
cowardliness.

Becoming God

Let's be clear, *I* led the procession down Front Street at four-thirty in the morning and was the first to hop the fence and scale the mountain. *I* took the green flag with the teddy bear imprint from its casing like King mother-fucking Arthur took Excalibur from that stone. And when I descended, I led my subjects across the street and the early morning traffic stopped in both directions to let us through.

I'm the one who got her while Kasey sat shirtless outside the bedroom door with a limp dick and read a Life magazine article about otters. And when her roommate broke down the door in tears and anger over the piss and maple syrup puddle in the living room I'm the one who took vengeance. Drove with inebriated clarity down the freeway while Kasey puked out the window. *I* got us home.

I'm the one who was choked by a cop in that smoky apartment while the others held me down until the ambulance arrived and the EMS brought up the stretcher. I'm the one who spoke to God, but in reality spoke to myself as they dragged me down the stairs, my arms and legs tethered to the stretcher and my head banged against every step.

I brought Austin back to life after the clowns danced outside the window in the backyard. All the while the obese hippie couple mashed their naked folds on top of one another on the trampoline, and their combined weight pressed the mesh into the grass beneath.

In every instance, in every attempt by the Devil to foil me, I have come out unscathed. I have come out the other side stronger. And If I come across angry, as a "vengeful God," or as an exaggerator or as vulgar to garner attention (which I am not), I hope you understand that it is only to emphasize the trials I have overcome to become who I am. To show you what I have gone through and come out as a savior. The Savior. Your Savior.

-ovich

-ovich
-ofsky
Born a Jew
Jealousy under a tree
Let's walk the neighborhood
Look at the beautiful lights
      And all I was
      Was cold.
      Jealous.
The generosity of that fat bastard
      And maybe, just maybe
      I was naughty.
And she hired me
at the Starbucks
I could work Sundays
Reba. Portly. Tight braids crimson
hair that bullshit
smile
Let the teenagers say "Frap" god
damn it
Well he's Jewish he told the girls
He had plans
Was studying to be a preacher
A good man
married at 18 to fuck
that's what they do.
Him and me, yeah

we could close down that Starbucks at
9 and have drink
in hand by 9:10.
He was alright
But he said well he's Jewish
and they screamed HEATHEN!
shoved the highlighted passages in my
face
put THE WORD OF GOD
          right there
          right there in my face
Aghast he watched
you know
he was true in his Judaic questions
          he just
          he just wanted to know
And they screamed
and he stood there
and I stood there
until they had exhausted voices
Disgusted they left whereas
they would have highlighted and
written notes
in God's word
blasphemy I considered
And he stood by the pastry case
          chocolate chip cookies
          marble loaf
          lemon loaf
          cranberry tarts

Shit, he cried
        I didn't know. I'm so sorry. I'm
so sorry.
9:08 we sat down at the bar
Buffalo Wild Wings East Beltline.
edge of the bar
First round on me
and he made sure to talk about
anything
except Judaism.
I hope he is well.
I hope he is happy.
I hope I'm still a Jew.

These Days Too

I got me a stepson
autistic got maybe a few sentences
20s now
only one taller than me
that I find shorter
but he – he's got it figured out
ain't gonna remember much about
you
three lines down
a thousand revolutions
we're down to five worth considering
two thousand and it's Jesus and the
periphery
three?
I got me a stepson
who knows that real living
is to be surrounded by bite-sized
candy
water sipped from a straw
animated cartoons
and a toy ray gun.

Compare Your Jesus

We have democratized the wretched
opinions of imbeciles to run amok on
the channel screens.
Garbage rivers flowing through bad
lighting and unearthly shit audio.
Portrait modes that, somehow, some
way, infiltrate the dirtiest of
pornography.
Handheld zooms that were infuriating
in 1987.
Everywhere we turn
Someone's life validated in a comment
box.
There is no merit here.
No consolation in the bits.
No sincerity that doesn't bleed into
something evil.
Ted was right, just ahead of his time.
And here we are.

Out Pondered the Hare

And when he thinks death
Under rain that lasts the day
Filtered through the rotted planks
above. Drip.
Drip. On the shoulder.
Ashes
Once wafted
Congealed into black goo
Where the soggy cotton
Was at once soft against the
fingernail
Hot against the throat
Out pondered
The hare's blinking eye. Drip.
Drip. On fur.
Every
thing
Beautiful.
Out pondered
the hare would be there tomorrow
Even if he was not.
And he would have no control over its
movement.

Its thoughts.
Its words
and that mortified him.

Don't Go Touching Them

"That's a bear," Leonard said as he
pointed to a squirrel.
Matty listened to his father and
nodded.

Decrepit camping chair
poked the dirt with a stick
hands tanned, dirt seeped deep
     the ridges of his skin
     on his shirt
     his jeans
     between his bare toes

The sun beat through trees
The late evening
     breeze cut woods.

"It is," Matty said, he knew better.
In the 2nd grade his class went on a
field trip to the zoo.
"Don't go touching them though,
there's the rabies."

Belly protruding out from under
a red and black flannel shirt.

Thumbed through an old
Sports Illustrated magazine.

"I won't touch 'em."

A dog's bark became summer
crickets.

Bathe in Bus Exhaust

Give me your hand
projected over bus exhaust
bent down
then crouched
Kippah secure
the calm morning
Backpack as Tzedakah
Pale skin through white collared

Speak softly in the morning rush
clink clink the coins
in a plastic cup
speak softly over deadlines
unforgiving debt
to-do lists

Bathe in bus exhaust
and build our lives
as passengers

Onward!

We sent her to her death in a white
Dodge Neon
spackled in street salt.
Onward! He commanded
after vomiting in the old snow.
She mustn't sit on his lap.
Mustn't run blood
Down
From her forehead
Onward! He thunk as he crawled
through the old snow. Thunk.
How we're overrated in thickets of
malcontents.
The drunks
and she lives in my skin
nestles into classrooms overrun by the
whites
in the fleeting winter sunlight.
Hazy today
he writes on his hand with his wet
finger.

Emotions Intimidated

Two men arrived
and emotions intimidated
    at first
Yet they, in time, did grow
to enjoy our company
    our wine
Though the well not deep
they drank
and when content
looked for lust
and the women noticed the desertion
from our common cause
and took to the angry stairs
the men slept in shifts
and at morning gold seeped
through
    the cracks
no longer violating trust
coldness subsided
and we laughed for an hour

Super Model Skin

Doesn't want to wake
with super model skin
coming off the needle
in the sun looking thin
with his wax paper brain.

Evening in a Crack House

I spent most of the evening
in a crack house basement
He parked his father's BMW on the
lawn

> and when he knocked
> on the front door
> they insisted I go
> to the basement

I was new
and new white people
are not to be trusted

My underworld companion was
gracious gave me a 40 of Olde English

We watched the Pistons
play basketball
on a black and white television

Johnny

Only a good guy with
As he hid under the desk a cacophony
of stale breath
/heartbeats

Told Mary about the good guy
her still with the salted blood spatter
drying
On her hoodie it was spirit day

    Go Falcons.

Went down to the corner store
and got herself a gun /red state
Got the two for one
got the explode inside you kinda shit

Yelled "faggot" as she pulled
He fell in a heap how the old shit
Went down/
Looked into his eyes

    Now we'll get free.

Curled up against her
she drove
Those American highways that just go

and go.
A hundred thousand miles plus on the
odometer
Hand-me-down
Maroon Volvo diesel
got that 80s almost 90s boxy feel.

He woke when the air felt warmer.
Hand-cranked the window
lit a cigarette
and gave a nod to the pavement.

That Stallion, That Beast

Stallion of creationism
Beast
Chicks on the side and
uncompromising
fury of whiskey filled invocations
She stuttered to his left and grunted –
the right

That moment as they lurched
As They Rolled
Lay waste in a gravel ditch

That stallion of creationism
That Beast
Disjointed prose and a monosyllabic
base
Jibber Jabber, he said
        [pause]
Is the greatest word [phrase] ever
created
        [pause]
20-minute soliloquy
on the proper use of y'all

definition history

several addendums

Watch him spittle Miller Lite
and in this moment, he sets his hand
on my shoulder
Steps in close
He whispers
        Spit on the devil Samuel
        Spit on him good
That Stallion.
That Beast.

Unnatural, a Tingle

Five in the morning,
Chicago April frigid.
Snow fell and settled on snow
packed down by tires muddy black.

A salt truck compacting the fresh
white with crunches
deserted streets,
their bright orange flashes
above
"Chicago Streets and Sanitation"
paint.

East on North Ave
right at Sedgwick,
under an elevated track

> "This is Sedgwick. Doors open
> on the right at Sedgwick."

No passengers
I exhaled
Sunday morning.

> "This is a Brown Line train to
> the Loop."

Maybe
if I tell them how it feels
that will be enough
to make it pass.

"This is Chicago. Doors open
on the right at Chicago."

Shit.
He sat right across from me
Sighed loudly
          with purpose
          with a preacher's intonation
Fit neatly into the contoured
plastic seat

Shit.
He looks like one of those cool
old Black men
that's got wisdom
cause he's seen it.

And he knew it.
Black derby hat
matted down his gray/white hair
pushed it out to the sides
Beard – tightly cropped
precision correspondence
with his hair.
Indigo pinstriped suit
Necktie rooted in similar blue
layered in pastel florals.
Hell – his shoes ebony.
Polished.
impeccable.
Wing-tipped.

Set a coffee leather satchel bag
on his lap

left his hands
atop the hide.

> "Looks like you're going
> somewhere, son,"

Ah, fuck.

> "But you aren't dressed
> for work, at least not none
> I can think of. It's Sunday
> morning. Early.

He waited
I cleared my throat.
He reclined slightly
I opened my mouth.

> "Quiet this morning,"
> he said.

> "This is Merchandise Mart.
> Doors open on the right at
> Merchandise Mart."

> "I'm heading to church."

I wondered
was it too early for church?

> "Now I know it's a little early
> for church. But I don't like to
> be rushed, never have been.
> See whether you're going

somewhere or praying, it ain't
no difference. See most people
just go and pray. They sing,
say the same thing every week.
Pastor gets up and tells a story.
Amen and done,"

"Lord Almighty I'm saved! And
then nothing until Sunday
rolls around again. Me, I like
to get to thinking about
praying before I pray. What
does it mean? What do I want
and what does the Lord want
from me? You know?"

A young Hispanic woman
pushed a stroller to the edge
lifted it slightly
boarded.

"Caution. The doors are
closing."

"Washington and Wells is
next. Doors open on the right
at Washington and Wells."

"It starts in the palms.
Damp. Unnatural."

"What does, son?"

"The devil."

"The devil?"

"Yes, please don't interrupt,
sir. If I stop he will win.
I need to tell you about him
and you need to listen
until my station."

"All yours, son."

"It starts in the palms. Unnatural.
A tingle,
originated just above the knees
and culminated at the groin.
Somehow the devil connects to the
heart the next beat
aggressive and deep,
as if speaking underwater.
That's when I know he's here.
Don't think that no else feels this.
Don't think that everyone is normal.
You are normal."

The Hispanic baby
began to cry

> "This is Washington and
> Wells. Doors open on the right
> at Washington and Wells. This
> is a Brown Line train to the
> Loop."

> "Come to church with me."

"No, sir. Thank you. That's where the
quiet is."

87

Constance

Constance
I told you I'd write you a poem
in 1996
Sitting with our legs dangling
off the top bunk
with an audience
below us
Tex was there
he can vouch for us.

James Colton, Jr.

18 years old
Caucasian
scrawny build.
Hair buzzed short, face clean shaven
sunken.
Caused his eyes to protrude slightly.

Born to James and Marie Colton
        (nee Marsh)
Pottstown, PA
Brother – twin, deaf, Timothy
Sister – Elizabeth
        (age 6)
James Sr. unemployed
Marie Colton KinderCare
He wants you to understand him,
his deaf twin brother.
He wants you to be his friend,
confide in his antics,
his love interests
in the bed of a pickup truck
with Bud Lights
in a vacant grocery store parking lot
facing the overgrowth
of a field.

Take Them Polaroids

C'mon my Baby
Light them candles
and take them Polaroids
in our electric-powered mobile home
on blocks
Pay sweet homage
to the click-clack heater
stuck out the faux wood veneer
Love our plasma TV
and Friends
the complete collection
on DVD.
We don't fight with our fists.
Not like them.
Not like them in #8.
#11.
Take them Polaroids baby
I'm gonna want our children
to know we've got it made.
When we get around to it,
when we decide
        [as a couple
        cause I love
        and respect you]
that we want to share
in our riches.

Advice from a Movie Star

Drove around for hours
primrose suburban cul-de-sac
Lost wake SUV dreams
Cordial to an ex-girlfriend
Pre-2009
Home tour tri-level with the dogs
a cat
Left cordial
Hoped for her to text
Idealized relations
I've maintained her Secret
in a drawer
Sometimes
After I dream of her
Idealized Her
I'll take off the cap
And smell the deodorant
While looking at her picture
And fight the ideal
Soap-scrubbed memories
Redacted auras those scenes thrown
at a wedding
Abortion recovery brought flowers
Weed night
Diet Coke day

Settled me into decrepit LA confines
Held me in darkness
the advice of a movie star

Hives in Motel Lobbies

Hives in motel lobbies
Glass bulletproof
Gulping Gin on hard mattress
Ex-Girlfriend awkward swiveling on
motel office chair
Gulping Gin while heater hums
12 degrees now non-smoking she
smokes
You too
Hug on entry
Hug on exit
Bookend physicality
Bar the pedestrian antics of ex-lover
spat
I need a shower she says
But not here
Yet even you think I'm beautiful
He tries
Buys me diamonds whenever he can

Hives in motel single suites
She bends over
He just wants her to leave
And let him continue to buy her
diamonds forever

A Morning Pilot

a morning pilot
someone to inflate my ego
remind me I am
a genius
flaws be damned
repetitive harm
that heartbeat erratic
from knowing wrong
lusting after what will go wrong
piercing disdain
odd flavors
of internet anonymity
fatness shoved behind keyboards
memories once jumped the heart
now muted
with cautious ex-lover repartee
send along a morning pilot
there's seething and discomfort
a jumping heart
for what I'm capable
of doing next

American Proper

This is where the pilots
and stewardesses would overnight.

Sleep.
Eat.
Drink.
Fuck.

Pressed neatly in oak veneer
branded carpet Pan Am subtle
throughout

and they let you take the drink
coasters home with you.

The women gave tours, dressed in
their Pan Am 1980s best - 1,500 euros
three hours.

I smoked a cigarette,
sipped whiskey on the balcony.

Berlin fog settled in, cloaked the
Mercedes Benz sign atop a building

distant, opaque.

"Women were down there bathing
nude when the sun was still up," a
Scandinavian man told me.

I peered over the edge
a greenhouse enclosed pool,
lit but empty.

"Were they hot?" I asked.

"Oh yeah, but far away so…"

"This is all new," he continued, staring
out into the distance, "they had to
rebuild everything after the war."

"Fuck 'em," straight up.

More American proper I could not be
without a cowboy hat.

Pianos, A Rare Find

His mother spoke rarely of religion,
which left discussions
void of any conflict
much of the time.

They rarely found time for church
except on required religious
occasions.

Ostracized to an extent
in the small town, but passersby
learned
to forgive
her petite hands ran across the keys
with such fluidity.

She taught Sam to play,
and Sam
in turn
assumed this talent would attract
pretty girls.
And while many wayward guitar lay
dormant
at country house parties
pianos were a rare find.

Shivering Mad Cold Quaking

The horrid – horrid stench
Shivering mad cold quaking
found warmth
resting against the chest
of some boy's girlfriend
wrapped in the layered glow
of her coat
feels like mass quantities
of hallucinogens
drugs on the fingertips
of dumb-shit glowstick hands

Businessmen in peacoats tucked away
in corners
in corresponding darkness
in stairwells

Found him in his eardrums
in the evolution halted forthwith
without the ability
to laugh

Heard balloons go
pop – pop – pop
Sucked down the aerosol smoke

before it filtered
before the lucidity of dream
fell apart
and the businessmen became
violently ill.

Shivering mad cold quaking
streaking across the valley
conceptual monsters
under blackness
that rendered all disasters
inevitable
impossible
those fertile virgin memories
metamorphic
into the barren collapsed lung
owed to new electronic products

Shivering mad cold quaking
we leave
I hear her father yelling at her
in Arabic
Her mother hit him
with a wooden spoon
and the yelling stopped
I sat down on the toilet seat
fully dressed
tried not to breathe
I just want to go home
I just want to go home

Royal Oak Street Corner October 30, 1999

My mother died
I just walked from 13 and Woodward
Fucked up
I can't believe those idiots
from Detroit had the nerve
to show up
tell *me* shit about *my* marriage
was annulled in 1985
Then that bastard married another
bitch whore
had two kids.

My mother died
it don't matter though
Eli will take care of it
We're starting a business
me and Eli
do you know Eli?

Oh, well, Eli's gonna take care of it
start a business
those fuckers
I can't believe
they showed up

My mother
Eli
Life's fucked up.

In Angelic Summer

Jesus man shave
wife-beater tattoos
sitting in a chair on the dirt looking
depressed
he needs a gun for our amusement
he needs a gun to shoot the girl
in angelic summer

S

Sprayed in color aqua
Suspicious
Screams at children praying
Playing
On bicycles
In Empty streets
Suburbia
Got him the walking stick
Playing
On scooters
Never hear a man
Scream
Like this man before
Watch him
Now
Listen that
Scratched voice
LPs on vinyl
From his front porch
Grassy lawn flowered
Never heard a man
Scream at children praying

Shatter Some Skulls

restraint, he said
grasping the aluminum
baseball bat
is the ideal
as is empathy
to be collected
to be able to breathe
in uncertain circumstances
is essential, he added
before lifting the bat
to his shoulders
I mean, look at them, he started
and then pointed
with the metal
a bunch of men, or should I say
boys
punching and kicking at each other
no place to run, really
stuck in the skinny driveway
between the two houses
stuck between
the two parked cars
we could yell out
ask them what it is
they are fighting about
and wait for the collective
realization

that none of them know
or
we could enter the fray
your bat
my bat
and shatter some skulls
the former, and he paused
to admire his soliloquy
would end this quickly
the latter
and we have ourselves
some fun

Blood Rotten Laced with Oil

Snuffed out
blood rotten laced with oil
antifreeze
They could have removed him
from the home
With pension, benefits
an alternative housing option
Spoke to him
in the manner of a fourth grader
Put their hands on his shoulder
Said good man you had yourself
Eloquence with a pen
Poignancy with a hammer
Cogency with a slow drawl
Insisted that yes, they could smell it too
blood rotten laced with oil
antifreeze
Set ablaze and
Plant nothing for the prairie's return
It is done and
To do something is human and
that would be the worst thing

Other books by Steven W. Simon

1200 Miles from Los Angeles

Ava in Lost Pines

bleach

Into the Fracking Fields

Red as Apple

stevensimonbooks.com

boundharepress.com